Into the Unknown

Written by Lynette Evans

U.S.A.

My name is Lori. I live in Florida, near Kennedy Space Center, where the space shuttles lift off. Do you know why astronauts are taller when they are in space than when they are on the ground?

Contents

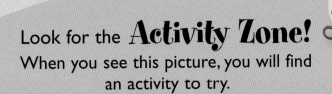

Look for the **Activity Zone!**
When you see this picture, you will find
an activity to try.

Searching the Sky

For centuries, people have been fascinated with the wonders that lie beyond our planet. When the first telescope was invented in the 1600s, an astronomer named Galileo Galilei used this new technology to study the stars and planets. Over the next few centuries, increasingly larger and more powerful telescopes were built, and people began to understand more and more about the universe.

Today's most powerful telescopes are used only by trained experts. However, a basic telescope can allow us to view the stars in much greater detail than we can see with the naked eye. Even a pair of binoculars provides greater magnification than Galileo had with his first telescope.

astronomer   a scientist who studies the planets, our galaxy, and the universe

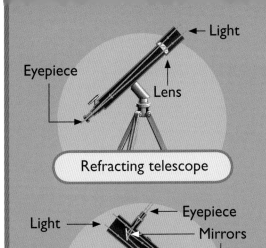

Light →
Eyepiece
Lens
Refracting telescope

Light →
Eyepiece
Mirrors
Reflecting telescope

Optical telescopes collect the light from distant objects and magnify it. There are two main types. Refracting telescopes use lenses to collect light, and reflecting telescopes use mirrors.

- **1610:** As a result of new telescope technology, Galileo announced that he had discovered four moons orbiting planet Jupiter. This proved the bold theory that not everything revolves around Earth.

- **1668:** Sir Isaac Newton invented the reflecting telescope, the first telescope to use mirrors. It magnified images thirty-five times.

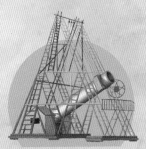

- **1781:** Sir William Herschel built a huge reflecting telescope. It was known at the time as a marvel of engineering.

5

Eye on Deep Space

Vibrating waves of energy, called *electromagnetic rays,* travel through space and matter. Light is the form of electromagnetic radiation that we can see and that we use to view space through optical telescopes. Other telescopes use computers to create images by detecting other types of electromagnetic rays, such as radio waves, infrared waves, ultraviolet rays, and x-rays.

Much of what we have learned about the universe in recent times has been gathered by telescopes that were carried into space in shuttles and left in orbit. Space-based telescopes can look deeper into space than Earth-based telescopes, because they are beyond Earth's atmosphere, which distorts incoming rays.

This is one of the many images taken by the Hubble Space Telescope. It shows light coming from a distant star called *V838 Monocerotis.*

distort to blur or twist something into another shape

Not all of the artificial satellites orbiting Earth look into the distant universe. Many look down on Earth. They are used to forecast the weather or to relay telephone, television, and Internet signals around the globe.

NASA launched the Hubble Space Telescope from the U.S. space shuttle *Discovery* in 1990. It is about the size of a school bus and orbits Earth every 97 minutes.

The Hubble Telescope has peered deeper into space than any other telescope. Directed by a team of experts at ground control in Baltimore, Maryland, it has taken over 700,000 images of cosmic events occurring in far corners of the universe.

When telescopes look far into space, they are also looking back in time. The images they capture are of moments in the distant past, because it takes a very long time for light to reach us from so far away.

Where Is Earth?

One of the first things that people used telescopes to study was our local solar system. We often think of Earth as huge, but compared with the size of the solar system, Earth is tiny. The Moon, which is our closest neighbor, is about 240,000 miles away! The Sun is about 93 million miles away. Earth is one of the planets that orbit the Sun. It is the third planet from the Sun and the only planet in the solar system that has the right conditions for life as we know it.

Our solar system is a tiny part of the Milky Way Galaxy—a brilliant spiral of space dust, gas clouds, and millions of stars. The Milky Way is just one galaxy in the millions of galaxies that make up the universe.

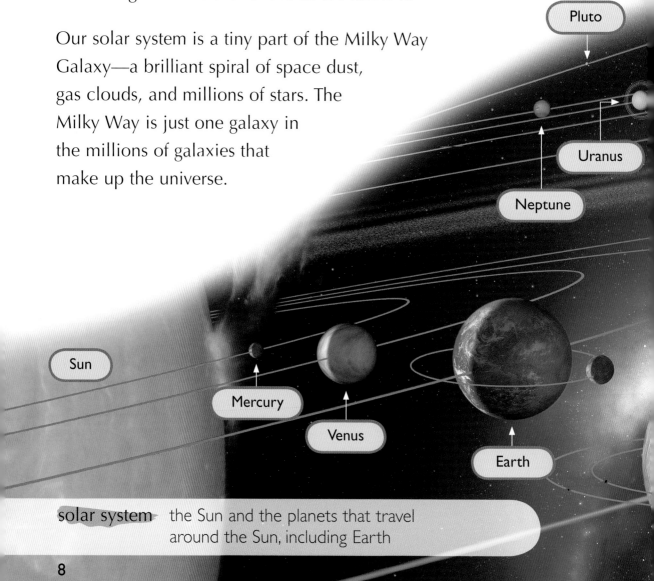

Pluto

Uranus

Neptune

Sun

Mercury

Venus

Earth

solar system   the Sun and the planets that travel
              around the Sun, including Earth

The Milky Way Galaxy

Saturn   Jupiter

THE SOLAR SYSTEM

Mars

Home, Sweet Home

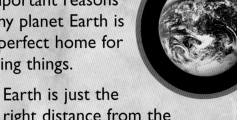

There are several important reasons why planet Earth is a perfect home for living things.

- Earth is just the right distance from the Sun for some water to exist in liquid form, not just as a gas in the air or frozen as ice.

- Earth has an atmosphere. It is surrounded and protected by a thin layer of gases—mostly oxygen and nitrogen. Earth's atmosphere creates our weather and provides oxygen for us to breathe.

- Earth spins around like a top, completing one turn every 24 hours. This rotation produces night and day.

Our nearest star, the Sun, is the center of our solar system. It provides all the light and heat needed for life. It is so large that a million Earths would fit inside it!

Sailing to the Stars

The more people looked into space and learned about it, the more they wanted to explore it themselves. By the second half of the 20th century, technology had reached a point where space travel became a very real goal.

In 1958, the U.S. created NASA (the National Aeronautics and Space Administration) with the aim of exploring space. In April 1961, Russian cosmonaut Yuri Gagarin became the first person to leave Earth's atmosphere and enter space. Inside a small spacecraft named *Vostok*, he orbited Earth in one hour, 48 minutes. Just 23 days later, NASA launched a rocket carrying astronaut Alan Shepard. He became the first American to travel in space, with a flight time of 15 minutes, 28 seconds.

NASA chose seven men to train as the first American astronauts. They were part of Project Mercury, the first U.S. space program to send people into space. Alan Shepard is in the back row at the left.

In the 1960s, people were fascinated with space travel. Astronauts and cosmonauts were seen as heroes. This Russian postcard celebrates Yuri Gagarin and important dates in the Russian space program.

In movies, spaceships zoom from star to star and galaxy to galaxy. In reality, however, Earth is a poor starting point for such space journeys. Scientists believe the nearest star to our Sun is about 25 billion miles away. A journey to this star at the speed of a jet airplane would take 4.8 million years! For now, space exploration occurs only within our solar system and in our imaginations!

People who fly on U.S. space missions are called *astronauts*, while Russian space explorers are called *cosmonauts*. Both words come from ancient Greek. *Astro* means "star," *cosmo* means "universe," and *naut* means "sailor."

Man on the Moon

Shortly after Alan Shepard's historic journey, U.S. President John F. Kennedy announced that the U.S. would strive to put a man on the Moon before the end of the 1960s.

The Russians sent many uncrewed missions to the Moon, achieving a number of firsts—first lunar orbit, first image of the Moon's far side, and more. Then in 1968, three U.S. astronauts on *Apollo 8* made the first crewed orbit of the Moon. At that time, this six-day flight was the longest on record. The next year, *Apollo 11* set an even more impressive record. Watched by millions of people around the world, U.S. astronaut Neil Armstrong became the first person to set foot on the Moon.

lunar   relating to the Moon

The Moon is a natural satellite of Earth. It is held in orbit by Earth's gravity. There is neither air nor water on the Moon. Its many craters were caused by volcanoes and by impact from rocks, called *meteoroids*, that travel through space.

Imagine you are setting up the first Moon base. Use construction paper, cardboard, aluminum foil, modeling clay, and any other craft materials to build a model Moon base. Include the following things.

1. Buildings where people can live, grow food, and conduct science experiments

2. A radio antenna for communication with Earth

3. Vehicles for exploring the Moon

4. A landing pad for spacecraft

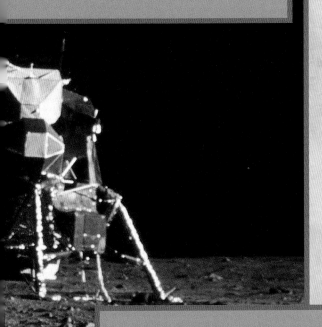

Apollo 11 astronauts Neil Armstrong and Edwin "Buzz" Aldrin spent two hours on the Moon. They collected rock samples and set up experiments. Their mission and safe return to Earth were great victories for science.

Rocket Power

Today, astronauts and their supplies travel into space in a reusable spacecraft known as a *space shuttle*. Most of the ride is smooth and turbulence-free. The most challenging moments occur during liftoff and on re-entering Earth's atmosphere.

To escape the powerful force of Earth's gravity, a space shuttle must reach a speed of 17,500 miles per hour. A rocket is the only type of engine powerful enough to attain this speed. At liftoff, rocket engines fire a space shuttle from zero to 100 miles per hour in just four seconds. The space shuttle keeps building speed until it reaches orbit.

The space shuttle *Atlantis* lifts off from Kennedy Space Center.

gravity   the force that pulls all objects toward large objects, such as planets and moons

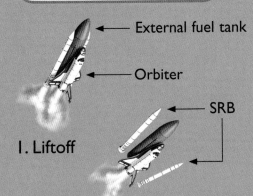

← External fuel tank

← Orbiter

← SRB

1. Liftoff

2. After 2 minutes, the solid rocket boosters (SRBs) use up all their fuel and parachute back to Earth.

3. After $8\frac{1}{2}$ minutes, the fuel in the external tank is used up. The tank falls away.

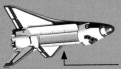

Payload doors

4. In orbit, the payload doors open, ready for work.

5. The orbiter must re-enter the atmosphere at a precise angle. If it is too shallow, it will bounce into outer space; if it is too steep, it will burn up.

The Force of Gravity

On Earth, gravity is the force that pulls everything toward the ground. Gravity also makes the Moon circle Earth and Earth circle the Sun. The strength of an object's gravity depends on the amount of matter from which it is made. The Sun is enormous and has a massive gravitational pull.

The force of Earth's gravity feels stronger the faster you speed up. During liftoff, astronauts experience a force of gravity that is three times stronger than usual. This makes it hard for them to move their arms and legs. In space, however, astronauts feel zero gravity and are weightless.

Thrills, Spills, and Ills

When the first astronauts were launched beyond Earth's atmosphere and into the unknown, no one knew if humans could survive in space. For these brave pioneers, the risk of death was part of the job, and the thrill of exploring new frontiers was worth the risk.

Today, astronauts are more knowledgeable about the journey ahead, but the job still comes with a fair dose of danger and discomfort. Space travelers often experience nausea and faintness as they adjust to being weightless. Without exercise, an astronaut's bones and muscles would weaken, because they are not working against gravity as they do on Earth. There are also some unexpected side effects from space travel. A person is taller in space than he or she is on Earth, because without gravity, the spine stretches out.

Eating in space is not easy, because food is weightless, just like everything else. If astronauts are not careful, their food can float away.

Outside the shelter of the shuttle, space is a sizzling 250°F in the direct sunlight and a freezing −250°F in the shade. A space suit prevents an astronaut from burning up or freezing. During a space walk, a life-support unit containing oxygen, batteries, food, water, and other supplies is carried in a backpack. A mini workstation containing tools is attached to the chest area. On Earth, the weight of the suit and supplies is usually heavier than the weight of the astronaut, but this doesn't matter in space.

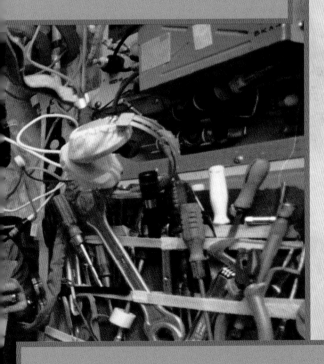

All astronauts must spend about two hours a day exercising. Here, astronaut Sharon Lucid is strapped in place so she can exercise without floating away.

17

Robots and Probes

Some of the most far-reaching discoveries about planets in our solar system have come from data sent back to Earth from uncrewed space probes and robotic rovers. These machines journey where no person has gone before. They are humankind's eyes and ears on distant worlds. Some make flybys only, others orbit planets and moons, and some touch down for land-based exploration.

The Jet Propulsion Laboratory (JPL) in California is NASA's center for robotic exploration of space. Scientists and engineers at the JPL build machines that can perform very complicated tasks millions of miles from home. Many machines never return to Earth, but the information they send back continues to build our knowledge of the solar system.

1. The probe separates from the orbiter.

2. The parachute opens.

3. Protective airbags inflate.

4. The lander hits the ground inside the airbags.

Spirit, a Mars rover, sends images of Mars back to Earth. In January 2004, NASA and JPL staff rejoiced as the first pictures of Mars and *Spirit*'s open lander appeared on their computer screens.

Several remote-controlled scientific vehicles, called *rovers*, have explored Mars. They reach the surface inside probes, which are fired out of orbiting spacecraft.

5. The airbags deflate, and the lander opens.

6. The rover leaves the lander.

Cassini-Huygens Mission

Nineteen nations worked together to build the Cassini-Huygens spacecraft. The Huygens space probe was launched from the Cassini orbiter on December 24, 2004, and 21 days later, it landed on the surface of Titan, Saturn's planet-sized moon. The Huygens probe has since spotted what seems to be an icy volcano on Titan. Scientists are especially interested in Titan, because it is the only moon in the solar system with a thick atmosphere that may be similar to Earth's atmosphere long ago.

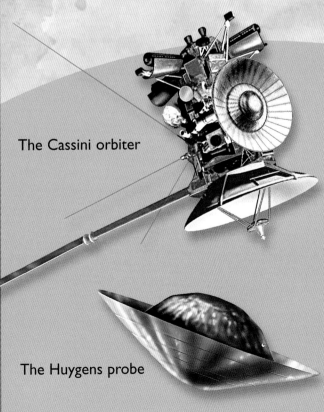

The Cassini orbiter

The Huygens probe

Building a Space Station

Until the first space station was launched in the early 1970s, humans had managed only brief visits into space. A space station provides both a permanent base camp and a space-based launching platform for ongoing space missions. Additionally, it allows scientists to study the long-term effects that living in space has on the human body.

In 1998, construction began on the *International Space Station (ISS)*, and today it continues to be built by astronauts from many countries. Because the station is in orbit and completes a lap of Earth every 90 minutes, adding sections to the *ISS* is a little like trying to put together a race car as it zooms around a track. Parts are brought up from Earth on shuttles and must be carefully attached without disrupting the station's orbit.

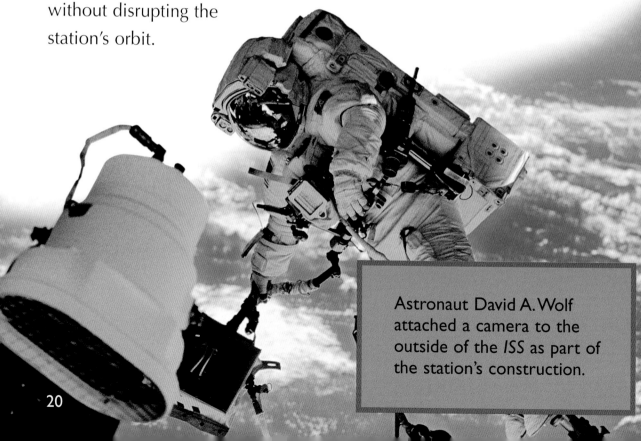

Astronaut David A. Wolf attached a camera to the outside of the *ISS* as part of the station's construction.

Mir, a successful Russian space station, was occupied almost continuously from 1986 until 2001. U.S. space shuttles were able to join, or "dock," onto the station.

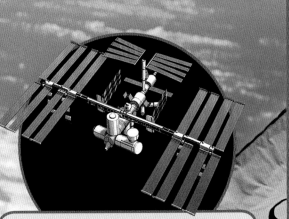

The *International Space Station*

Space Junk

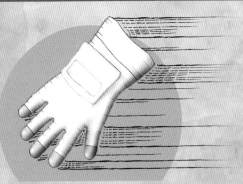

One of the greatest threats to the *International Space Station* is the danger of collision with space debris, or junk, traveling at extremely high speeds. Space junk is made up of old, human-made objects in orbit around Earth. These may be used rocket parts, broken satellites, or even lost clothing or equipment, such as an astronaut's glove or a dropped camera. Without air to break down the trash, it remains intact and in orbit forever.

Antarctica is a place on Earth where the temperature is too cold for trash to break down. Laws now protect this fragile environment so that trash is not carelessly discarded. Should this happen in space?

Close Encounters

You don't have to be an astronaut to share in the discoveries of new worlds and the wonders beyond our planet. Everyone can enjoy the night sky, and if you visit an observatory, you can look through giant telescopes to study the stars and planets.

Space camps offer children a chance to experience firsthand what it's like to be an astronaut. Campers learn how it feels to be weightless, what it's like to work in a space suit, and how to solve problems both from ground control and in the pilot's seat.

The most popular space-camp activities often involve simulators. These machines are a little like amusement-park rides. They mimic the feelings of liftoff, walking on the Moon, and zero gravity.

simulator   a machine that imitates a real experience in safe conditions

The number of stars you can see in the night sky depends on where you live. If you live in a city, glare, or "light pollution," from city lights will block your view of fainter stars.

Kennedy Space Center

NASA's John F. Kennedy Space Center at Cape Canaveral, Florida, is America's number-one spaceport and a gateway to the universe. It prepares the shuttles for each mission, operates each countdown, and manages landing and recovery activities. Visitors can tour the Space Center, watch shuttle launches, explore the history of America's space program, and learn about NASA's latest missions.

Find Out More!

1. Find out about the latest images being beamed back to Earth from telescopes in space. What are scientists learning from these images?

2. Robot probes are constantly sending new images and information about other planets back to Earth. Find out about a recent discovery.

To find out more about the ideas in *Into the Unknown*, visit www.researchit.org on the web.

Index